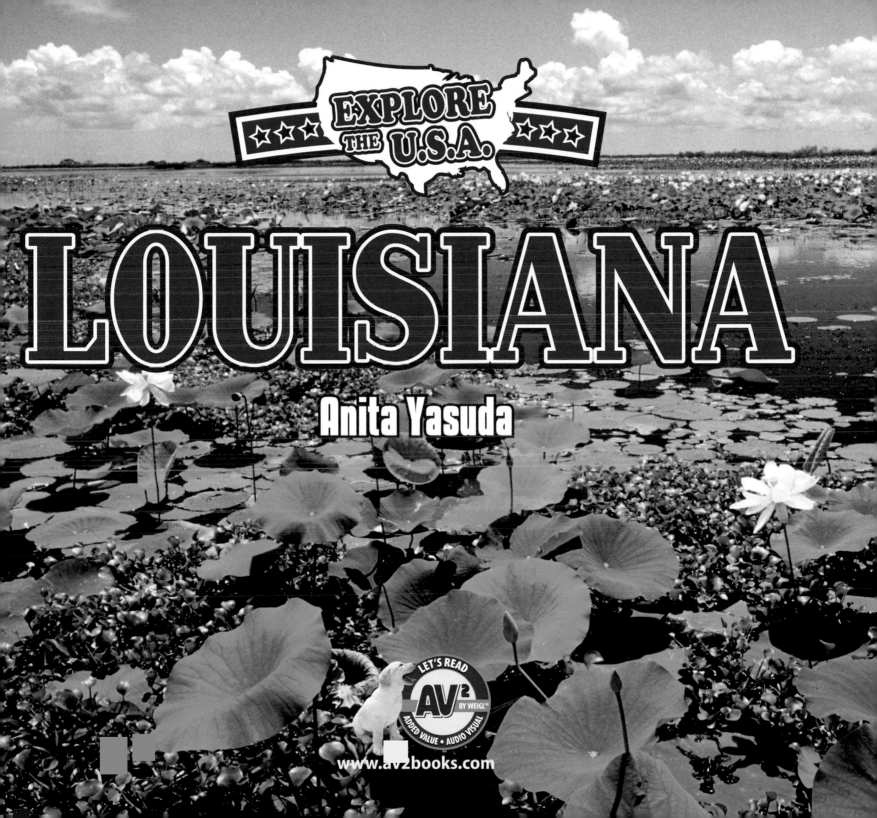

EXPLORE THE U.S.A.

LOUISIANA

Anita Yasuda

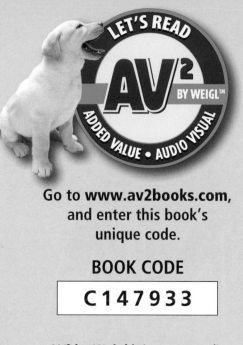

AV² provides enriched content that supplements and complements this book. Weigl's AV² books strive to create inspired learning and engage young minds in a total learning experience.

Your AV² Media Enhanced books come alive with...

Audio
Listen to sections of the book read aloud.

Video
Watch informative video clips.

Embedded Weblinks
Gain additional information for research.

Try This!
Complete activities and hands-on experiments.

Key Words
Study vocabulary, and complete a matching word activity.

Quizzes
Test your knowledge.

Slide Show
View images and captions, and prepare a presentation.

... and much, much more!

Go to **www.av2books.com**, and enter this book's unique code.

BOOK CODE

C147933

AV² by Weigl brings you media enhanced books that support active learning.

Published by AV² by Weigl
350 5th Avenue, 59th Floor
New York, NY 10118
Website: www.av2books.com   www.weigl.com

Library of Congress Cataloging-in-Publication Data
Yasuda, Anita.
 Louisiana / Anita Yasuda.
   p. cm. -- (Explore the U.S.A.)
 Includes bibliographical references and index.
 ISBN 978-1-61913-355-6 (hard cover : alk. paper)
 1. Louisiana--Juvenile literature. I. Title.
 F369.3.Y37 2012
 976.3--dc23
                        2012015066

Printed in the United States of America in North Mankato, Minnesota
1 2 3 4 5 6 7 8 9 16 15 14 13 12

052012
WEP040512

Project Coordinator: Karen Durrie
Art Director: Terry Paulhus

Weigl acknowledges Getty Images as the primary image supplier for this title.

LOUISIANA

Contents

3

This is Louisiana.
It is called the Pelican State.
Pelicans are large birds
that live in Louisiana.

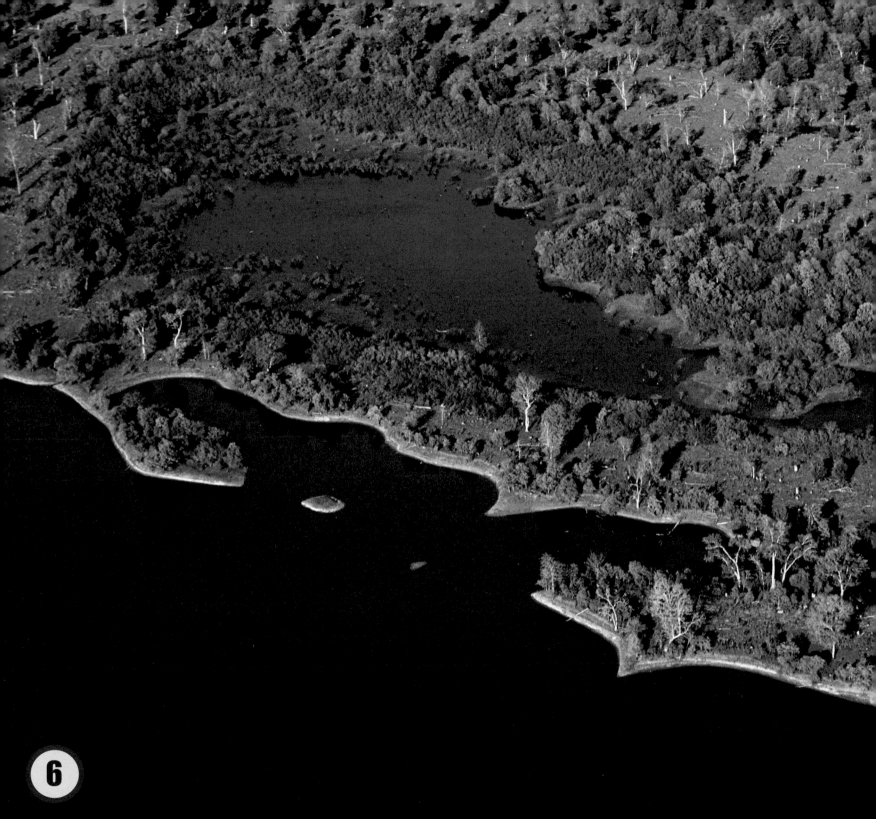

This is the shape of Louisiana. It is in the south part of the United States. Three other states border Louisiana.

Where is Louisiana?

N
W • E
S

Canada

Pacific Ocean

United States

Atlantic Ocean

Mexico   Gulf of Mexico

Louisiana is next to the Gulf of Mexico.

Louisiana was once owned by France. The land was called New France.

Many places in Louisiana still have French names.

⑩

The magnolia is the state flower of Louisiana. Magnolias grow on trees.

The Louisiana state seal has a pelican with three chicks.

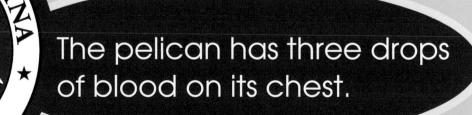
The pelican has three drops of blood on its chest.

This is the state flag of Louisiana. It has the same picture as the state seal.

UNION JUSTICE CONFIDENCE

The mother pelican on the flag is feeding her chicks.

The state bird of Louisiana is the eastern brown pelican. Its beak can hold up to 3 gallons of water and fish.

A pelican can spread its wings 10 feet wide.

This is the state capital of Louisiana. It is a city named Baton Rouge. Its name means "red stick."

Ships come to Baton Rouge through the Mississippi River.

Oil is found in Louisiana. Some of this oil is under the ocean. Oil can be made into gas for cars.

Louisiana makes enough gas to fill 800 million cars each year.

Louisiana is known for its festivals.

New Orleans has a big party each year. People dress in costumes and watch a parade.

21

LOUISIANA FACTS

These pages provide detailed information that expands on the interesting facts found in the book. These pages are intended to be used by adults as a learning support to help young readers round out their knowledge of each state in the *Explore the U.S.A.* series.

Pages 4–5

Louisiana is nicknamed the Pelican State for the birds that live along its Gulf Coast. The French explorer Robert Cavalier, Sieur de la Salle, claimed the Louisiana territory in 1682 for King Louis XIV of France. Louisiana is named after the king.

Pages 6–7

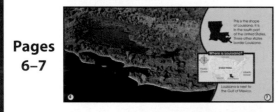

On April 30, 1812, Louisiana became the 18th state to join the United States. Louisiana shares its borders with Arkansas to the north, Mississippi to the east, Texas to the west, and the Gulf of Mexico to the south. Louisiana is at the mouth of the Mississippi River, which flows into the Gulf of Mexico. Louisiana's southern coast has one of busiest commercial waterways in the country.

Pages 8–9

Louisiana became part of the country in 1803 when the United States bought the land from France in the Louisiana Purchase. The price was less than three cents per acre for 828,000 square miles (2,144,520 square km) of land. This treaty doubled the size of the United States.

Pages 10–11

The magnolia became the official state flower in 1900. Magnolia trees can grow up to 80 feet (24.4 meters) tall. The first governor of Louisiana, William C.C. Clairborne, admired the pelican and wanted its image included on the seal. The pelican's blood represents self-sacrfice.

Pages 12–13

The Louisiana flag was adopted in 1912. The design shows the pelican and its chicks from the state seal. Around the pelican is the Louisiana motto, "Union, Justice, and Confidence."

Pages 14–15

The eastern brown pelican was named the state bird in 1966. A pelican has a large pouch under its bill that it uses to scoop fish out of the water. In the 1970s, pelicans became an endangered species due to the use of pesticides along the Gulf Coast. After measures to protect their habitat, pelicans are no longer endangered in Louisiana.

Pages 16–17

Baton Rouge is on the Mississippi River. Although Baton Rouge is hundreds of miles (km) from the ocean, the river has been dredged so that large ocean-going ships can dock there. Baton Rouge has the ninth-largest port in the United States. The city's name is French and means "red stick."

Pages 18–19

Oil was discovered in Louisiana in 1901. Oil drilling and refining then became a major source of income for the state. Today, the oil industry in Louisiana produces billions of gallons (liters) of gasoline. Louisiana is among the top five oil-producing states. One oil refinery in Baton Rouge produces half a million barrels per day.

Pages 20–21

The annual party in New Orleans is called Mardi Gras, which means "Fat Tuesday." The celebration was brought over by European settlers. The first Mardi Gras parade in New Orleans was in 1857. People wear colorful clothing, march in street parades, and ride on floats. More than two million people fill the streets of New Orleans during Mardi Gras.

KEY WORDS

Research has shown that as much as 65 percent of all written material published in English is made up of 300 words. These 300 words cannot be taught using pictures or learned by sounding them out. They must be recognized by sight. This book contains 63 common sight words to help young readers improve their reading fluency and comprehension. This book also teaches young readers several important content words, such as proper nouns. These words are paired with pictures to aid in learning and improve understanding.

Page	Sight Words First Appearance
4	are, in, is, it, large, live, state, that, the, this
7	next, of, other, part, three, to, where
8	by, have, land, many, names, once, places, still, was
11	a, grow, has, its, on, trees, with
12	as, her, mother, picture, same
15	and, can, feet, up, water
16	city, come, means, river, through
19	be, cars, each, enough, for, found, into, made, makes, under, some, year
20	big, people, watch

Page	Content Words First Appearance
4	birds, Louisiana, pelican
7	Gulf of Mexico, shape, United States
8	France, New France
11	blood, chest, chicks, drops, flower, magnolia, nest, seal
12	flag
15	beak, eastern brown pelican, fish, wings
16	Baton Rouge, capital, ships, stick
19	gas, ocean, oil
20	costumes, festivals, New Orleans, parade, party